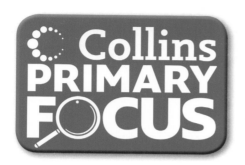

Spelling
Pupil Book 4

Joyce Vallar and Carol Doncaster

William Collins' dream of knowledge for all began with the publication of his first book in 1819. A self-educated mill worker, he not only enriched millions of lives, but also founded a flourishing publishing house. Today, staying true to this spirit, Collins books are packed with inspiration, innovation and practical expertise. They place you at the centre of a world of possibility and give you exactly what you need to explore it.

Collins. Freedom to teach.

Published by Collins
An imprint of HarperCollins*Publishers* Ltd.
77–85 Fulham Palace Road
Hammersmith
London
W6 8JB

**Browse the complete Collins catalogue at
www.collinseducation.com**

Text, design and illustrations © HarperCollins*Publishers* 2011

Previously published as *Collins Focus on Spelling*, first published 2002.

10 9 8 7 6 5 4 3 2 1

ISBN: 978-0-00-742659-1

Joyce Vallar and Carol Doncaster assert their moral right to be identified as the authors of this work.

British Library Cataloguing in Publication Data
A Catalogue record for this publication is available from the British Library.

Cover template: Laing and Carroll
Cover illustration: Q2A Media
Series design: Neil Adams and Garry Lambert
Illustrations: Shirley Chiang, Nick Duffy, Kevin Hopgood, Kerry Ingham, Claire Mumford, Andy Robb, Sarah Wimperis

Printed and bound by Printing Express Limited, Hong Kong.

Contents

Unit   Page

1   **Unstressed vowels in multisyllable words**   4

2   **Prefixes from other languages**   6

3   **Suffixes as a support for spelling**   8

4   **The suffixes** *-ary*, *-ery* **and** *-ory*   10

5   **The suffixes** *-ive*, *-ance* **and** *-ence*   12

6   **Tricky words (1)**   14

Progress Unit 1   16

7   **Tricky words (2)**   18

8   **Words from other languages (1)**   20

9   **Words from other languages (2)**   22

10   **Tricky words (3)**   24

11   **Spelling rules (1)**   26

12   **Spelling rules (2)**   28

Progress Unit 2   30

Spellchecker   32

Unstressed vowels in multisyllable words

Which is the unstressed vowel in words like *teacher* or *camera*?

Every syllable has one vowel sound.
This may be a single vowel (*a*, *e*, *i*, *o*, *u*) or *y* or two vowels which make one sound.
Some vowels are hard to hear in words.
These are called unstressed vowels.

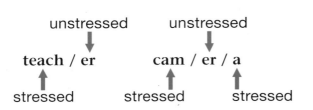

Getting started

Copy these words.
Mark the syllables.
Circle the unstressed vowel in each word.
The first one has been done to help you.

1. vegetable → veg/(e)/ta/ble

2. temperature   3. seven

4. button   5. sister

6. pedal   7. husband

8. pupil   9. happening

10. interest   11. excellent

12. quarrel   13. external

More to think about

Each of these words is missing an unstressed vowel.
Write the words correctly.
Underline the unstressed vowel.
The first one has been done to help you.

1. gardner ➔ gard<u>e</u>ner   2. mystry

3. busness   4. numbr

5. immedate   6. nursry

7. considr   8. intrest

9. breakfst   10. cardign

11. famly   12. childrn

Now try these

Two vowels coming together often make one sound, for example *rain*.
However, sometimes when two vowels come together they make two sounds,
for example *dial*.
If you say the word slowly, pronouncing each vowel, it is easier to hear
the unstressed vowel.

1. **Copy these words.**
   Mark the syllables.
   Circle the unstressed vowel.
   The first one has been done to help you.

   a) diamond ➔ di/ⓐ/mond

   b) violent   c) medium

   d) familiar   e) cruel

   f) fuel   g) poem

   h) valuable   i) obedient

   j) casual   k) fluoride

   l) sanctuary   m) jewellery

2. **Choose three words from Question 1 and use each one in a sentence.**

Prefixes from other languages

Did you know that some prefixes in the English language come from other languages?

The English language has been added to by many ancient languages. Understanding the origin of words can help you to understand their meaning.

Getting started

Latin has influenced the English language.

Latin prefix	Meaning	From it we get ...
aqua-	water	aquarium
audi-	hear	auditorium
super-	above/greater	supersonic
trans-	across/through/beyond	transport

Use a dictionary to find at least two words for each prefix.

Prefix	Word	Meaning
aqua-	aquarium	a glass fish tank
audi-		
super-		
trans-		

More to think about

Ancient Greek has influenced the English language.

Prefix	Greek word	Meaning	From it we get ...
aero-	aer	air	aeroplane
micro-	mikos	small	microphone
tele-	tele	far	telegraph

1. Use a dictionary to find at least three words for each prefix.

Prefix	Word	Meaning
aero-	aeroplane	a flying vehicle
micro-		
tele-		

2. Choose three of your words from Question 1, each with a different prefix.
   Use each word in a sentence.

Now try these

1. What do these words mean?
   Check your answers in a dictionary.

   a) octopus → an eight-legged sea creature

   b) binoculars

   c) octahedron

   d) bikini

   e) bilingual

   f) octagon

   g) binary

2. The prefixes *oct-* and *bi-* are both prefixes from the ancient world.
   What do these prefixes mean?

3. Find two more examples of prefixes that indicate numbers.

Suffixes as a support for spelling

What is a suffix? What does it do? Let's look at some common suffixes.

A suffix is a group of letters added to the end of a word that changes its meaning.

visit + or = visitor

Getting started

1. **Add a suffix from the box to make a new word.**
   You can use each suffix more than once.
   Check the new words in a dictionary.

-ism	-let	-like	-wise	-or	-wards	-er	-ish	-some

   a) direct → director   b) for

   c) child   d) inspect

   e) trouble   f) clock

   g) print   h) book

   i) vandal   j) like

   k) farm   l) back

   m) magnet   n) quarrel

   o) life   p) fight

2. **Choose nine of the words you made in Question 1, one for each suffix.**
   Write a definition for each of the nine words.

More to think about

1. **Add two different suffixes to the root words to make new words.**

Root word	Useful suffixes	+ Suffix 1	+ Suffix 2
play	-ment	played	playfully
instruct	-ing		
act	-ed		
hope	-tion		
race	-or		
friend	-fully		
hand	-ly		
like	-less		
	-ship		
	-ness		

2. **Make a list of other suffixes that you know.**
   Can any of them be added to the root words in Question 1?
   Write any new words you can make.

Now try these

Choose one set of three words from your table in *More to think about*.
For example: play ➡ played ➡ playfully
Use each word in a sentence.

The suffixes *-ary*, *-ery* and *-ory*

Let's look at the suffixes **-ary**, **-ery** and **-ory**.

The suffixes **-ary**, **-ery** and **-ory** can sound very similar and are often confused.

Always check your spelling of words using these suffixes if you are not sure.

Getting started

Add the suffix *-ery* to the root words to make new words.
You may need to change the spelling of the root word.
Check your answers in a dictionary.

Root word	Root word + *-ery*	Root word	Root word + *-ery*
nurse	nursery	rob	
jewel		slip	
bribe		cook	
join		bake	
brew		machine	
scene		pot	
brave		slave	

More to think about

1. Finish each word to name the pictures.
   Each word ends in *-ary* or *-ory*.
   Check your answers in a dictionary.

a)

libr_____

b)

fact_____

c)

conservat_____

d)

dormit_____

e)

secret_____

f)

Febru_____

2. Work out the answers to these clues.
   Each word ends in *-ary* or *-ory*.
   Check your answers in a dictionary.

   a) a television programme giving information
      about real people and events ⟶ d_____

   b) the study of the past ⟶ h_____

Now try these

1. These words end in *-ary*, *-ery* or *-ory*.
   Some of them have been spelled wrongly.
   Write the misspelled words correctly.

✓cookery	delivary	sanctuary	ordinery	necessery
secretery	granary	tributory	anniversory	laboratory

2. Choose five words from Question 1 and use each one in a sentence.

The suffixes *-ive*, *-ance* and *-ence*

Let's look at the suffixes **-ive**, **-ance** and **-ence**.

A suffix is a group of letters added to the end of a word that changes its meaning.

secret + ive = secretive

appear + ance = appearance

correspond + ence = correspondence

Getting started

1. **Add the suffix *-ive* to make a new word.**
   Remember, you may need to change the spelling of the root word.
   The first one has been done to help you.

   a) distinct → distinctive   b) prohibit

   c) expense   d) suggest

   e) pass   f) digest

   g) extent   h) decorate

   i) success   j) impress

   k) product   l) progress

2. **Choose five words from Question 1 and use each one in a sentence.**

3. **What happens to the word *explode* when you add the suffix *-ive*?**
   Write the new word.

More to think about

The suffixes *-ance* and *-ence* are often confused.
Choose the correct spelling of each word.

1.	performence	performance
2.	disappearance	disappearence
3.	dependence	dependance
4.	circumference	circumferance
5.	evidance	evidence
6.	importance	importence
7.	confidence	confidance
8.	disturbance	disturbence
9.	presence	presance

Now try these

Write the root words.
Remember, the root word may have changed when the suffix was added.
The first one has been done to help you.

1. a) creative ➔ **create**
   b) active
   c) inventive

2. a) comprehensive
   b) constructive
   c) effective

3. a) reference
   b) difference
   c) occurrence

4. a) grievance
   b) inheritance
   c) resemblance

Tricky words (1)

Can you think of ways to remember how to spell tricky words like *aerial*?

A **mnemonic** is a way of remembering the spelling of a tricky word.

aerial   **a**ngry
           elephants
           ride
           in
           amber
           lorries

Sometimes it helps you to remember how to spell a word if you can picture the mnemonic.

Getting started

1. **Copy these words.**
   Underline the part of the word that the mnemonic helps you to remember.
   The first one has been done to help you.

   a) <u>is</u>land   An island is land.

   b) separate   There is a rat in separate.

   c) believe   Don't believe a lie.

   d) soldiers   Soldiers sometimes die.

2. **Funny mnemonics that you make up yourself are often the easiest to remember.**
   Make up mnemonics for these tricky words.

   a) tongue   b) cough

   c) amateur   d) previous

More to think about

Here are two more mnemonics.

difficulty   Mr **D**, Mr **I**

               Mr **FFI**,

               Mr **C**, Mr **U**

               Mr **LTY**!

rhythm   **r**hythm

              has

              your

              toes

              hopping

              madly

Make up a rhyme or a mnemonic to help you remember these tricky words.

1. elephant
2. beautiful
3. friend
4. because
5. guest
6. necessary

Now try these

These strategies will also help you to spell tricky words.

a) pronouncing silent letters: for scissors say **s – c – issors**

b) exaggerating syllables: **ab – so – lute – ly**

c) finding words within words: **col*our*ful**

Which strategy would you use to help you remember these tricky words?

1. lieutenant
2. conscience
3. abscess
4. quarantine
5. definite
6. discipline
7. rhubarb
8. meringue
9. vicious
10. skeleton

Progress Unit 1

**A. Copy these words.
Circle the unstressed vowels.**

1. traveller
2. peculiar
3. reasonable
4. difference
5. temporary
6. sickening
7. miserable
8. discovery
9. unusual
10. diary
11. separate
12. reference

B. Choose a prefix from the box to make a new word.

| aero- | trans- | super- | tele- | bi- | micro- | aqua- |

1. _____scope
2. _____natural
3. _____vise
4. _____atlantic
5. _____dynamic
6. _____chip
7. _____lung
8. _____monthly
9. _____wave
10. _____space
11. _____text
12. _____tic

C. Add a suffix to each word to make a new word.
Remember, you may need to change the root word.

1. trouble
2. child
3. clock
4. after
5. book
6. respect
7. bake
8. educate
9. journal
10. buy
11. back
12. quarrel

D. Write these sentences again, spelling the underlined words correctly.

1. The woman wore sparkling jewellory.

2. The couple celebrated their anniversery.

3. The secretery typed very quickly.

4. She checked the spelling in a dictionery.

5. Scamp was no ordinery dog.

6. He rushed off to the laboratery.

7. The new car was extraordinery.

8. They ate their lunch in the refectary.

9. The umbrella was necessery as it was raining.

Can you think of more ways to remember how to spell tricky words like *necessary*?

Here are some different strategies to help you remember tricky spellings.

- Say the word slowly and exaggerate the pronunciation.
- Use the "Look, Say, Cover, Write, Check" method.
- Look for smaller words within big words.
- Make up your own mnemonics.
- Always use a dictionary to check.

Getting started

1. **Write the correct spelling of each word.**
   Think of a strategy to help you remember the correct one.

a) embarassed	embarrased	(embarrassed)
b) necessery	necessary	neccesary
c) parallel	parralel	parrallel
d) acommodation	accommodation	accomodation
e) possesses	posesses	posseses
f) occasional	ocassional	occassional

2. **Use each correctly spelled word in a sentence.**

More to think about

These words can be difficult to spell.
Saying the words slowly and exaggerating the pronunciation will help you.

Copy the words.
Mark the syllables.
Underline the unstressed vowels.
The first one has been done to help you.

1. temperature → tem/p<u>e</u>r/<u>a</u>/ture

2. innumerable
3. cemetery
4. deodorant
5. maintenance
6. intermediate
7. similar
8. lenient
9. gradual
10. desperate
11. February
12. literacy
13. memorable
14. correspond
15. financial

Now try these

A **mnemonic** is a way of remembering the spelling of tricky words, like this:

because
Big
elephants
can't
always
use
small
exits.

1. **Invent a mnemonic to help you remember the spelling of each word.**

   a) biscuit
   b) definite
   c) hygiene
   d) excellent
   e) friend
   f) percentage

2. **Now illustrate one of your mnemonics.**

Words from other languages (1)

Why do the letters **ch** make different sounds in the words *chaos* and *chute*?

In words that come from the **Greek language**, the letters **ch** can make the sound **k**.

mechanical   chaos   stomach

In words that come from the **French language**, the letters **ch** can make the sound **sh**.

chute

Getting started

1. **Write a word to name each picture.**

    a)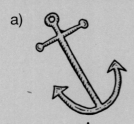

    anchor

    b)

    c)

    d)

2. **Work out the answers to these clues.**
    Check your answers in a dictionary.

    a) a group of people who play musical instruments together   ____ch_____

    b) a group of people who sing together   ch_____

    c) the fictional people in a film, play or book   ch_____

More to think about

1. **Work out the answers to these clues. Check your answers in a dictionary.**

   a) a wooden house with a sloping roof, in a mountain area or a holiday camp

   ch_____

   b) a leaflet which gives information about products or services

   _____ch_____

2. **Write a word to name each picture.**

   a)

   b)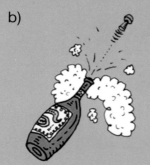

   c)

   d)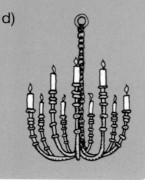

Now try these

Use *ch*, *c* or *sh* to fill each gap.
Write the complete sentences.

1. The accident at the traffic lights __aused __aos.

2. At __ristmas the __ildren sang __arols in the __athedral.

3. The __alendar dates are arranged in __ronological order.

4. The __over for the ma__ine is on the __elf.

Words from other languages (2)

Why do the letters **ph** make the sound **f** in words like *physics*?

In words that come from the **Greek language**, the letters **ph** make the sound **f**.

physics

phrase

phoenix

Getting started

1. **Write a word to name each picture.**
   a)

alphabet

   b)

   c)

   d)

   e)

   f)

2. **Work out the answers to these clues.**
   Each word has the letters ph in it.
   Check your answers in a dictionary.

   a) a punctuation mark used to join words together   hy_____

   b) another name for a ghost   _____tom

   c) words on a tomb about a person who has died   epi_____

   d) a mythical monster with a lion's body and human head   s_____nx

More to think about

Complete the words containing *ph* in these groups.

1. clarinet	trombone	sa___ph____
2. cousin	niece	n__ph___
3. giraffe	rhinoceros	e____ph____
4. biology	chemistry	phy_____
5. comma	full stop	apo____ph__
6. cube	triangular prism	sph_____

Now try these

1. **Join words from the box to make seven new words.**
   You can use each word more than once.
   One has been done to help you.

photo	graph	auto	tele	copier	graphy	copy	grapher

   photo + grapher = photographer

2. **Some of the new words belong to the same word family.**
   How many word families can you find? Write the words in family groups.

Tricky words (3)

Can you think of ways to remember how to spell tricky words like *advice* and *advise*?

The text around the word indicates the correct spelling.

I need some good *advice*.

I would *advise* you to try again!

Noun	Verb
advice	advise
practice	practise

I need some good advice.

I would advise you to try again!

Getting started

Remember: *ice* is a noun and ***advice*** and ***practice*** are nouns, too.

Complete these sentences using *advice*, *advise*, *practice* or *practise*. The first one has been done to help you.

1. The brass band was told it needed to <u>practise</u>.

2. I left the house early on your _____.

3. The dental _____ is closed at the weekend.

4. The lawyer will _____ her client on his defence.

5. Cleaning your teeth after every meal is good _____.

6. Louise should _____ every night before the competition.

7. The teacher gave the students good _____ on how to study.

8. I would _____ you not to drive in these treacherous conditions.

More to think about

altar is a noun

to *alter* is a verb

These words are sometimes confused. Using different strategies will help you to remember how to spell them.

An altar is a raised table in a church.

Altar has *ta* in it for *table*.

Think of some strategies to help you remember how to spell these words. Write down your strategies.

1. stationary   stationery

2. lose   loose

3. course   coarse

4. council   counsel

Now try these

Choose a word from the box to complete each sentence.

council   counsel   altar   alter
coarse   course   stationary   stationery
lose   loose

1. The joiner used _____ sandpaper to smooth the wood.

2. The seamstress will _____ the length of my coat.

3. The student wore _____ clothing for karate.

4. The children voted to elect the new members of the school _____.

5. The runaway lorry hit a _____ bus.

Spelling rules (1)

What other spelling rules are useful to learn?

- **q** is always followed by **u** in the English language

- **ti** and **ci** are the two spellings most frequently used to say **sh** within a word

- **si** is used when the **sh** sound is voiced:

  invasion

- **cede**, **ceed** and **sede** are easily confused, but **cede** is used most often at the end of a word:

  precede

Getting started

1. **These words can be tricky to remember.**
   Use the "Look, Say, Cover, Write, Check" method to learn how to spell them.

   a) quite   b) quiet   c) quench   d) quadrilateral

   e) qualification   f) quaver   g) quay   h) query

   i) queue   j) quiche   k) quotation   l) questionnaire

2. **Choose two words from Question 1 and think of a mnemonic for each one.**

3. **Choose two words from Question 1 with more than one syllable. Mark the syllables.**

More to think about

1. **Complete these words using *ti*, *ci* or *si*.**

   a) man___on

   b) an___ent

   c) pa___ent

   d) infec___ous

   e) musi___an

   f) na___onal

   g) divi___on

   h) gra___ous

   i) finan___al

   j) par___al

   k) inva___on

   l) consulta___on

2. **Write out the words that contain the letters *ti* again. Mark the syllables.**

Now try these

1. **The letter strings *cede*, *ceed* and *sede* are often confused. Complete and learn this rule to help you to remember which to use.**

   - The three **ceed** words are: suc*ceed*   ex_____   pro_____

   - The one **sede** word is: super_____

   - All other words use **cede**:   pre_____   re_____

2. **Use a dictionary to check the meaning of each word.**

3. **Choose three of the words and use each one in a sentence.**

Spelling rules (2)

What should you remember when you add a suffix to a root word?

If a word ends in a consonant + **y**, change the **y** to **i** before adding a suffix, except for the suffix **-ing**.

cry → cried → crying

If a word ends in **-e**, drop the final **e** before adding a vowel suffix (like **-ing** or **-ed**) or **y**. Keep the **e** before adding a consonant suffix (like **-ly** or **-ness**).

bake → baked → baking
late → lately → lateness

If a word ends in a single **l** after a short vowel, double the **l** before adding the suffix.

signal → signalling

Getting started

1. **Add as many suffixes from the box as you can to make new words.**

-ing	-y	-ly	-able

   a) like   b) shake   c) value   d) move

   e) excite   f) migrate   g) shine   h) love

2. **Add -able to these words to make new words.**

   a) replace   b) notice   c) charge   d) manage

More to think about

Add as many suffixes from the box as you can to make new words.
You will not be able to add all the suffixes to each word.

| -es | -ness | -ed | -ly | -er | -ing |

1. heavy   **2.** pretty   **3.** carry   **4.** supply

5. funny   **6.** busy   **7.** trendy   **8.** bury

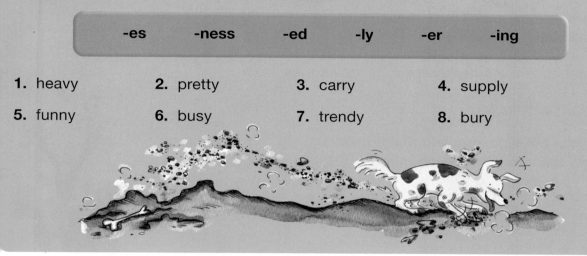

Now try these

1. Add the suffix to the root words.

a)
| signal |
| stencil | **-ing** |
| tunnel |

→ *signalling*
→
→

b)
| panel |
| pedal | **-ed** |
| cancel |

→
→
→

2. Choose one suffix from the box to add to each word.

| -ic | -ist | -er |

a) medal

b) metal

c) travel

Progress Unit 2

A. Work out the answers to these clues.
Each word contains *ch*.

1. arranged in the order in which things happen   ch_____

2. a state of disorder   ch_____

3. a piece of fabric attached to a person to allow them to fall safely from an aircraft   _____ch_____

4. a part of a song which is repeated after each verse   ch_____

5. a large group of musicians   ___ch_____

6. a sparkling white wine made in France   ch_____

7. the reflection of sound   ___ch_____

8. a booklet that gives information about a product or service   _____ch_____

B. Work out the answers to these clues.
Each word contains *ph*.
Check your answers in a dictionary.

1. a machine which makes instant copies   ph_____

2. the 26 letters from A to Z   ___ph_____

3. words on a tomb about the person who has died   _____ph

4. the signature of a famous person   _____ph

5. a great fear or hatred of something   ph_____

6. a chart showing number information   _____ph

7. your sister's or brother's son   _____ph_____

8. a large long-tailed game bird   ph_____

C. Add a suffix from the box to make a new word.
   You may need to drop a letter or double a letter before adding the suffix.

| -ure | -ive | -ance | -ence |

1. assure

2. mass

3. decorate

4. exist

5. attend

6. insure

7. excel

8. product

9. interfere

10. please

11. press

12. impress

D. Complete these sentences.

1. I need to _____ every day before the competition.
   (practice, practise)

2. My sister is about to _____ her first tooth.
   (loose, lose)

3. The coach will _____ the children about the best running shoes to buy.
   (advise, advice)

4. Chicken was served as the main _____.
   (coarse, course)

5. Paper, pens and other writing equipment are called _____.
   (stationary, stationery)

6. The drought had a disastrous _____ on the people.
   (effect, affect)

Spellchecker

Write these signs correctly.
Check the spellings in your dictionary.

1. Broshure of .... speciality orcids

2. Documentery vandlism – the way forward

3. Jewelry Sail

4. Charlie's Sircus Daily Performences

5. Airobatic Display 10 a.m.

SK8

7. Williamswell practise Surjery Hours

6. Fieldway + farmacy +

9. quew hear for tikkets

8. Next parashute jump 2 p.m.

10. Favourible intrest rates

11. Bransfield Counsel Comittee Meating Room 7